NO MORE DIAPERS!

NO MORE DIAPERS!

BY JOAE GRAHAM BROOKS, M.D.

AND MEMBERS OF THE STAFF OF THE BOSTON CHILDREN'S MEDICAL CENTER

PICTURES BY JOHN E. JOHNSON

A Merloyd Lawrence Book
DELTA/SEYMOUR LAWRENCE

A MERLOYD LAWRENCE BOOK
Delta Books/Seymour Lawrence Edition
Published by
Dell Publishing Co., Inc.
1 Dag Hammarskjold Plaza
New York, New York 10017

Delta ® TM 755118, Dell Publishing Co., Inc.

ISBN: 0-385-29308-9 (previously ISBN: 0-440-06508-9)

Reprinted by arrangement with Delacorte Press/Seymour Lawrence
Printed in the United States of America

9 8 7 6 5 4 3 2

Introduction for Parents

In our society young mothers often find themselves very much alone as they face the tasks of rearing their children. Some tasks loom larger than others, but few have been as stressed and overstressed as toilet training.

Many women reject the methods of their own mothers as too rigid and old-fashioned. They hesitate to bother busy pediatricians with their questions, and are sometimes even reticent to ask a friend for advice when their efforts seem unsuccessful. In search of the right approach they read the latest books and articles. Armed with this sometimes conflicting information, they march into what may become the first real conflict between them and their child.

This book, with its two very simple stories, is designed to offer a mutually reassuring approach to what can be a trying period. Your child will probably be between one and a half and two and a half years old when you read it to him. Some children are more difficult to train and may be a little older. One story is for boys, the other for girls, so that any child can identify with the main character. In this way the child's attention remains focused on the theme of bowel and bladder control without being diverted by the introduction of sexual differences.

The purpose of the stories is to help make clear to your child what this process is all about, what you expect of him, and what is the goal of his training. At the beginning it is difficult for a very young child to have any real understanding of what toilet training is all about. The stories depict the pride and happiness of a child as he achieves control over his body and feels more grown up.

It is not always easy for mothers to communicate to their children what they want of them. The child who has not yet been toilet-trained has no real experience of the comfort and pleasures of being clean, dry and more independent. He is apt to be resistant, if not downright opposed to giving up the pleasure of being in diapers.

For the very young child being in diapers has certain comforting aspects. The diaper is warm, soft and familiar, and he can relieve his discomfort whenever he wishes while wearing it. He doesn't have to tolerate the distress of a full bladder or bowel or disrupt what he is doing in order to sit on something cold, hard or strange. He isn't at all concerned about dirtiness or cleanliness, and his mother's approval has had no connection up to this time with how or when he relieves himself.

The initiation of training is often seen by the child as an abrupt and unwelcome intrusion on his familiar habits. He has no way of knowing the satisfaction he might derive from the development of new habits. Toilet training is a dramatic example of the important process of giving up childish pleasures in order to enjoy more mature privileges and feelings of pride and accomplishment.

You are probably all too aware of the fact that certain aspects of training can affect the child's personality development and his ways of getting along with other people as he grows older. In this process of training the child is asked to develop inner controls over his own impulses. It isn't an easy task for him, but as he progresses, he experiences a sense of mastery over his own body. These feelings are very important and helpful to him as he gradually becomes more self-sufficient and mature. They add to his self-esteem and begin to overcome the opposite feelings of helplessness and smallness inevitably felt by young children.

If you respond with approval and pleasure to his successful sessions on the potty and with tolerance and patience to his inevitable lapses, he will feel that he is basically a worthwhile person and that you have faith that he can accomplish what you have asked him to do. If, on the other hand, his efforts and failures are met with reactions of disgust, anger or punishment, he may look upon his body and its products as something bad or unacceptable. This kind of experience, especially if it is a repeated one, can lead to basic feelings of inferiority and worthlessness that may persist for a lifetime.

A child's sense of his ability to meet challenges and carry out tasks required of him is profoundly influenced by his mother's attitude during toilet training. If you can be relaxed and convey the idea that you believe in his eventual success, he will feel heartened in spite of his initial and to-be-expected "failures." We often hear a child, when confronted with a task in a classroom or on the playing field, express the feeling that he "can't do it." He may cling stubbornly to this conviction despite the urging and reassurance of the adults around him. Once this kind of conviction gets established in the child's mind, it is extraordinarily difficult to modify it. I cannot emphasize strongly enough how important it is to bolster the child's feeling that he "can do it!"

A young child is by nature a very self-centered being. He believes the world revolves around him, and his body is the center of that world. It is vital for him to know that his body is good and valued by others. Remember that his body excretions are seen by him as parts of himself. The idea that urine and feces are unpleasant or dirty are learned reactions, not natural ones. If you can try to keep these negative notions to yourself, it will be very helpful to your child. Too often a child develops the impression that if his urine and bowel movements are bad things to be gotten rid of as quickly as possible, then his body must somehow be bad, too.

It is necessary to make clear by frequent and clear reminders just what you want him to do. Sometimes mothers worry so about starting up a conflict with the child that they really don't guide and help him enough during training. This lack of resolution on the mother's part may arouse frustration and exasperation and prolong the whole process. The repeated reminders need to be matter-of-fact but not fiercely insistent. If the training is too rigid and fussy, the child can emerge as an individual who is never satisfied unless everything is "just so," spotless, and in absolute order. These anxious and compulsive pursuits take much time and energy that could be directed into more gratifying and productive avenues as the child grows and develops.

The way a child reacts to your efforts to toilet-train him, to your requirements of him during this time, may affect the way he will react to other authority figures as he grows older. After the repressive Victorian era, many American parents went to the other extreme and were too hesitant about making clear to their children what their expectations were. They found it difficult to set limits on their children's behavior for fear of installing neurotic inhibitions in them. This may be one of a number of reasons why we now see so many children who have poor control over their own impulses and little respect for any authority. A middle-of-the-road course is best. Reasonable, helpful rules which are clearly set forth and are accepted by both parents and children help the child to build up inner controls and become a more sociable adult. A person with such inner controls shows respect for authority figures later in life but maintains his capacity to rebel against unjust constraints.

Regular times for meals, for getting dressed and undressed, for going to bed and for toileting give the young child a sense of regularity and predictability in his daily life. From this reasonable regulation he gets the feeling that he is not a helpless creature buffeted about by forces he cannot control.

A child who gets the feeling from his mother during the toilet-training process that his body and its products are acceptable and basically good, that he can succeed in spite of his occasional failures, that he can achieve mastery over his body's urges, that life can be predictable and ordered, and that people in authority over him can be reasonable, reliable and just, is well on his way toward maturity. We hope that these two stories will shorten the training period and make it easier and more enjoyable for both you and your child.

Joae Graham Brooks, M.D.
Assistant Clinical Professor of Psychiatry,
Harvard Medical School;
Staff, Beth Israel Hospital

Suggestions to Mothers About Toilet Training

Before you launch your child into a program of toilet training, it is helpful to think through some of your own feelings about it. It cannot be denied that your attitudes and some of your own childhood experiences will affect the way you train your child. For example, a mother who has strong feelings about cleanliness will find it harder to live with the ups and downs of the training process, especially if she connects virtue with cleanliness.

There are many outside pressures to get a child out of diapers at as early an age as possible. Grandmothers, neighbors, friends, even husbands, are prone to announce that they certainly had thought "that child would be dry by now." It is easy to transfer the pressure onto a child who isn't quite ready to accomplish control. When there is this external pressure, it is more difficult to be patient and tolerant of the child's inevitable lapses. Children sense anxiety in their mothers and may absorb some of it, thereby making the process more difficult for all concerned. Instead of seeking advice from others, mothers often would benefit more from listening to their own inner judgment when deciding whether or not the child is ready to have a new demand placed on him.

There usually are other pressures, too. Perhaps there's another baby on the way or a move to a new neighborhood in the offing, or perhaps the desirable nursery school will take only children who are trained. Since toilet training is inevitably somewhat stressful, it is wise not to impose it on a child at a time when he may be under other pressures as well.

Toilet training is the first step in the child's development at which the mother must depend on *his* cooperation to accomplish *her* goal. Even very young children realize this, so it is helpful to begin when things are generally harmonious between mother and child. If there is friction or conflict, and the mother is overeager, this sets **the stage** for trouble: the child frustrates her by not cooperating. **Mother**s who feel very strongly about keeping strict control may find this time a little **threatening** for them.

Boys are often slower to train than g**irls.** In general they seem to be a little slower to take developmental steps. **All** very young children see their bowel movement as a part of their own body. Some may worry that if this material can be so easily flushed away, perhaps other parts of them could

disappear, too. Boys have more anxiety about this than girls and may, therefore, be more fearful of the whole process and require a little more patience.

Some boys take pride in standing at the toilet and directing the stream of urine into the bowl. It is important to encourage the boy to hold his penis to direct the stream properly, for if you hold it for him it doesn't help him become more grown up and self-sufficient and may prolong the training process. A step stool at the toilet may help.

It is the child's wish for his mother's love and approval that motivates him to cooperate with her requests. Her acceptance and approval gradually come to mean more to him than the pleasures of being in diapers. Enthusiastic approval and the pleasure a mother shows in her child's accomplishments are clear to him. He will be pleased and proud, too.

It is very important not to scold or punish the child for his lapses in toilet training. Harshness may increase his fear and resentment. His wish to avoid or turn away from an unhappy experience will only make the endeavor more difficult and prolonged. Praise him for his success. Although it isn't always easy, be calm about his failures. You can help him most with patience, encouragement, and a gentle reminder that "next time" he'll remember.

The best time to begin toilet training is when your child begins to remain dry for longer and longer periods of time, and when he shows some sign of being aware that he needs to empty his bladder or bowel. This usually occurs between the age of one and a half and two and a half years. On the one hand, it is best not to press him until he shows some sign of readiness. If you do, a struggle may ensue simply because he does not understand the meaning of this activity that seems to restrict his freedom.

On the other hand, it is not helpful to let a child go on untrained beyond the time when he is ready. Prolonging his babyhood robs him of the important feelings of achievement which help him in his progress toward maturity.

Often a child feels more comfortable and secure on a potty chair, because his feet are on the floor. Having to sit on a seat on top of a toilet with its noisy flushing mechanism frightens some children.

At the beginning of the training process, a young child needs regular reminders to sit on the potty chair. He is not yet always aware of the periodic fullness of his bladder and bowel.

Some mothers prefer to have the child sit briefly on the potty chair every couple of hours during the day in the hope of encouraging him to establish a routine. This scheduling may work for some but not for others. Ten minutes at a time is long enough for a very young child to sit. We do not encourage giving the child toys or books while he is on the potty for they will only distract his attention and energy from the task at hand.

Training pants can be used if you wish. They are quicker and easier to take down than a pinned diaper. They give your child the definite impression that he is growing up. If he has an accident while wearing training pants, he'll be immediately aware of it! You may, however, be doing more laundry in the beginning. And there may be puddles.

Dryness at night usually comes a little later, but occasionally a child may stay dry all night simultaneously with daytime control. Diapers can be used at night until the child shows a definite ability to control his bladder during the day. Then it is important to have him sleep without the diaper at night. Otherwise, he may assume you expect and are giving him

permission to wet his diaper. In this way, you may unwittingly delay dryness at night.

The wish for approval and the tendency to want to imitate older brothers and sisters are positive motivating forces for the child. Letting a small child watch a brother or sister urinate may prove helpful. Because the child's body is so small in comparison with an adult's and because there are differences in the way adult male and female bodies appear, watching a parent may cause feelings of inferiority or anxiety. This should not be encouraged.

Sometimes a child of two or a little older becomes very agitated and upset if efforts are made to toilet-train him. If this happens, it is best to reassure him that it is all right, that he doesn't have to do it now, and to give him a respite of a few months.

In spite of all this fanfare and discussion, most children do not present real problems. The training period rarely takes more than a few months and is almost never as difficult as you've been led to believe. If you wait until the child seems ready, if you show patience with his failures, pride in his successful efforts and are consistent in your ways of dealing with him, the process should go along well. You will both share the pride that comes from reaching important goals.

How To Use The Stories

The attention span and the ability to comprehend new and complex information varies tremendously between the ages of eighteen months and three years. This is a period in which important progress in learning and development takes place. For this reason we suggest that you use only the illustrations for a younger child, and explain the pictures in familiar language you know he can understand. The text can be read to the older ones who are able to grasp more facts. Use your own judgment as to what your child seems ready and able to deal with.

Adult terms for the body's excretions are used in these stories, for it is known that young children *can* learn correct words just as easily as childish ones and it is wise for children to learn early the correct names for things. However, we urge you to feel free to substitute terms which you may like better and with which you and your child may be more familiar. As with all children's stories, you may find that you are asked to read this one over and over again. With each reading your child will probably identify more and more with Susie or Johnny and the important developmental steps they are making.

NO MORE DIAPERS FOR JOHNNY!

Johnny is a little boy.
He is two years old.
Here he is.

He lives in a tall building
with his Mommy and Daddy
And his big brother, Mike.

Here they are.

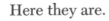

Johnny wears diapers.
He likes them when they're dry
Because they feel soft and warm.
Here is Johnny in his diaper.

Do you wear diapers, too?

But Johnny doesn't like his diapers
When they get wet.

Here is Johnny looking sad
Because his wet diapers
Don't feel good anymore.

Johnny's Mommy told him
About a little chair
That has a pot under it.
It is called a potty chair.

She said
That little boys and girls
Sit on a potty chair
So that they can put their urine*
And their bowel movements*
In the pot.
Then their diapers feel
Nice and dry.

*More familiar words may be substituted here.

Johnny's Mommy asked him
If he would like to have
His big brother's potty chair.

Johnny said, "Yes!
I want Mike's potty chair."

So Johnny and his Mommy
Went down to the basement
And looked for the potty chair.
"Here it is!" said Johnny's mother.
"Now it is yours."

Then they went back upstairs
And took his potty chair
To the bathroom.

Here is Johnny's potty chair.
Do you see the pot under it?

Do you have a potty chair?

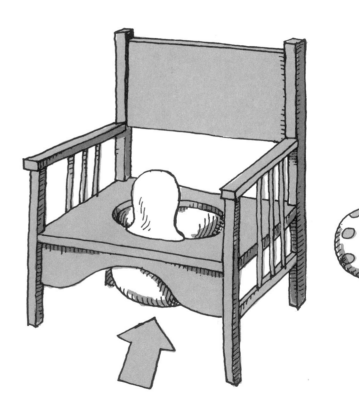

Johnny sat down on his potty chair
With his diaper on.
It was a nice chair,
So he sat on it a lot

Then one day he sat on the potty chair
With no diaper on.
At first the chair felt a little cold.
Then it felt fine again.

One day
When Johnny was sitting on his potty chair
Some urine came out of him
And went into the pot under his chair.
It made a funny little noise.

Johnny's Mommy was happy.
She said, "That's very good, Johnny!"
She had a big smile on her face.
Johnny was happy, too.

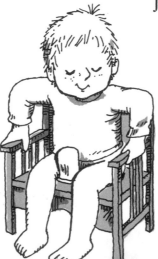

Then Johnny took the pot
With his urine in it
And put his urine
Into the toilet.

Johnny turned the handle on the toilet.
The water came and took his urine away.
"Goodbye, goodbye!" said Johnny.
He and his Mommy laughed.

After that
Johnny put his urine in the pot
A lot.

One day his big brother
Stood in front of the toilet
And put his urine into it
Standing up.

Johnny wanted to be grown up like Mike
So he stood in front of his potty chair
And put his urine right into
The pot.
That was fun.

Johnny put his bowel movements
Into the pot, too.
He took them to the toilet
And flushed them away.

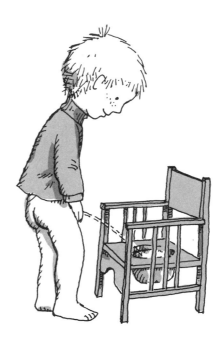

Once in a while Johnny forgot
To put his urine
Or his bowel movement
In the pot.
Then his diaper didn't feel good
Anymore.

The next time, Johnny remembered
To put it in the pot.
Then he felt much better.

Johnny's Mommy told his Daddy
How Johnny kept his diaper dry.
His Daddy was happy and proud.
"Good for you, Johnny," he said.
And he smiled a big smile.

Now Johnny's diapers stay dry.
So he can wear underpants, just like the ones
His big brother, Mike, wears.
Here is Johnny in his new underpants.

Johnny is happy.
His Mommy and Daddy are happy, too.
No more diapers for Johnny!
He's a big boy now.

And do you know what?
You can do what Johnny did.
Then think what a big boy
You'll be!

NO MORE DIAPERS FOR SUSIE!

Susie is a little girl.
She is two years old.

Here she is.

She lives with her Mommy and Daddy
In a little white house.

Here they are.

Susie wears diapers.
She likes them
Because they feel warm and soft.
Here is Susie in her diaper.

Do you wear diapers, too?

One day Susie's diaper
Got very wet.
The wet diaper didn't feel nice
Anymore.
Susie didn't like the wet feeling
At all.

Here is Susie
Looking sad
Because her wet diaper
Doesn't feel good.

Susie's Mommy told her
About a little chair
With a pot under it.
It is called a potty chair.

Her Mommy said that
Little boys and girls
Sit on a potty chair
And put their urine*
And their bowel movements*
In the pot.
Then their diapers
Feel dry and good.

*More familiar words may be substituted here.

Susie's Mommy asked Susie
If she would like to have
A potty chair of her own.
Susie said, "Yes!"

So Susie and her Mommy got in the car and
Went to a store.

There a man found
A little white potty chair
For Susie.
Here it is.
See, there's a pot under it.

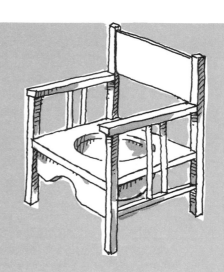

There were toidy seats
In the store, too.
They go on top of the toilet
And you sit on them.

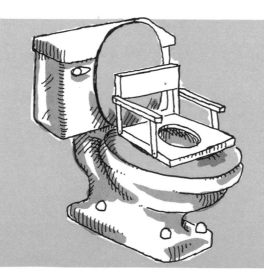

Do you have a potty chair?
Or do you have a toidy seat?

When they got home,
Susie sat down on her potty chair
With her diaper on.
She liked her chair,
So she sat on it
A lot.

One day she sat on it
With no diaper on.
It felt a little cold.
Then it felt fine.

All of a sudden
Some urine came out of Susie
And went into the pot
Under her chair.
It made a little noise.

Susie's Mommy was happy
When Susie's urine
Went into the pot.
She said, "Good for you, Susie!"
And her Mommy smiled a big smile.
So Susie was happy, too.

Then Susie took the pot
With her urine in it
And she carried it to the toilet.
She put her urine
Out of the pot
Into the toilet.

Then she turned the toilet handle.
The water came in
And took her urine away.
"Goodbye, goodbye!" said Susie.
She and her Mommy laughed.

After that
Susie put her urine
In the pot
Quite a lot.
After a while
She put it in
Whenever she wanted to.

Susie put her bowel movements
In the pot, too.
She flushed them down the toilet
The same way.

Sometimes
Susie forgot
To put her urine in the pot.
Then her diaper got wet and cold
And didn't feel good.

Next time
Susie put it in the pot again.
Then she felt better.

Susie's Mommy told her Daddy
How Susie kept her diaper dry
A lot.
Her Daddy was very proud of her.
"What a big girl you are, Susie,"
He said.

Susie's diaper didn't get wet
Anymore.
Susie's Mommy said that
She could wear underpants now,
The way big girls do.

So Susie and her Mommy
Went to the store again.
They bought some pretty underpants
For Susie to wear.

Susie and her Mommy went home.
She took off her diaper and
Put on her new underpants.
Here she is
In her new underpants.

Susie is happy.
Her Mommy and Daddy are happy.
No more diapers for Susie!
She is a big little girl now.

And do you know what?
You can do what Susie did.
Then think what a big girl
You'll be!

About the Author

JOAE GRAHAM BROOKS, M.D., is a child psychiatrist in private practice and on the staff of the Beth Israel Hospital. She is also Assistant Clinical Professor of Psychiatry at the Harvard Medical School. Dr. Brooks is the mother of two daughters.

About the Illustrator

JOHN E. JOHNSON is a well-known illustrator of children's books. His work has been included in shows of the New York Society of Illustrators and the American Institute of Graphic Arts. Mr. Johnson is the father of two children.